IT'S TIME TO EAT TANGELOS

It's Time to Eat
TANGELOS

Walter the Educator

Silent King Books
A WhichHead Entertainment Imprint

Copyright © 2025 by Walter the Educator

All rights reserved. No part of this book may be reproduced in any manner whatsoever without written per- mission except in the case of brief quotations embodied in critical articles and reviews.

First Printing, 2024

Disclaimer

This book is a literary work; the story is not about specific persons, locations, situations, and/or circumstances unless mentioned in a historical context. Any resemblance to real persons, locations, situations, and/or circumstances is coincidental. This book is for entertainment and informational purposes only. The author and publisher offer this information without warranties expressed or implied. No matter the grounds, neither the author nor the publisher will be accountable for any losses, injuries, or other damages caused by the reader's use of this book. The use of this book acknowledges an understanding and acceptance of this disclaimer.

It's Time to Eat TANGELOS is a collectible early learning book by Walter the Educator suitable for all ages belonging to Walter the Educator's Time to Eat Book Series. Collect more books at WaltertheEducator.com

USE THE EXTRA SPACE TO TAKE NOTES AND DOCUMENT YOUR MEMORIES

TANGELOS

The tangelos are ripe and sweet,

It's Time to Eat
Tangelos

A citrusy snack that's fun to eat!

Round and orange, they shine so bright,

It's time for tangelos, what a delight!

Peel the skin, so soft and thin,

Let the juicy fun begin!

Tiny sections, neat and round,

Bursting with flavor, the best around.

The smell is fresh, so zesty and clean,

Like sunshine from a fruity dream.

Each bite is tangy, sweet, and tart,

Tangelos bring joy to every heart.

They grow on trees, so tall and fair,

In sunshine's glow and loving care.

Farmers pick them, one by one,

So we can enjoy their fruity fun.

It's Time to Eat
Tangelos

Packed with vitamins, oh so grand,

Tangelos help us feel strong and stand.

A snack that's healthy, tasty too,

Perfect for me, perfect for you!

In a salad or on their own,

Tangelos make their sweetness known.

Squeeze the juice or eat them whole,

Tangelos surely warm the soul.

They make us smile, they make us cheer,

The tangelo season's finally here!

Let's share with friends, let's share with all,

Tangelos bring fun, big or small.

The trees are buzzing with busy bees,

Helping grow our tangelo trees.

It's Time to Eat
Tangelos

Nature's teamwork, so great to see,

A tasty gift for you and me!

So grab a tangelo, don't delay,

It's the perfect snack to brighten your day.

With every bite, remember the treat,

Tangelos are special, juicy, and sweet!

When the season's done, don't feel blue,

Tangelos will come back for you!

Until then, let's give a cheer,

It's Time to Eat
Tangelos

To the tangelo, the fruit we hold dear!

ABOUT THE CREATOR

Walter the Educator is one of the pseudonyms for Walter Anderson. Formally educated in Chemistry, Business, and Education, he is an educator, an author, a diverse entrepreneur, and he is the son of a disabled war veteran. "Walter the Educator" shares his time between educating and creating. He holds interests and owns several creative projects that entertain, enlighten, enhance, and educate, hoping to inspire and motivate you. Follow, find new works, and stay up to date with Walter the Educator™

at WaltertheEducator.com

www.ingramcontent.com/pod-product-compliance
Lightning Source LLC
LaVergne TN
LVHW052016060526
838201LV00059B/4046